Heights Of Life

Heights Of Life

Tanmoy Bhattacharjee

HAWAKAAL PUBLISHERS

Heights of Life
A collection of Poems
by Tanmoy Bhattacharjee

First Edition : November, 2015

© Tanmoy Bhattacharjee

Cover Design : Bitan Chakraborty

Published by Bitan Chakraborty, on behalf of Hawakaal
from 185, Kali Temple Road, Nimta, Kolkata-700049
E-mail : hawakaal.pb@gmail.com
Contact : +91 9088029197

Printers : Shanti Mudran, Pataldanga Road, Kolkata-9

ISBN : 978-81-931958-19

Rs. 200

I dedicate this book to my living gods—

Shri Dhananjoy Bhattacharjee (Baba)
Smt. Ila Bhattacharjee (Ma)

Baba, your disguised faith and ready support made this book possible.

At least you were there, Ma...

Foreword

Reading a new poem has always been a thrilling experience. As a child I would wait for my father's return from office, and as he stood at the door – tired – yet he smiled (at a later stage I understood it was a worn out one with the marks of the entire day) the most brilliant of smiles. So I understood father twice, the second time deeper.

In the same manner, reading a poem for the first time gives a similar experience. However, reading it a second time opens the doors of nuances. The surface floats somewhere but within the outer folds of poetry lie the hidden layers of an aanchal – the folds of the end of a sari. And when you contemplate on each and every fold, new wisdom surfaces up.

Likewise, Tanmoy Bhattacharjee's debut collection of poems Heights of Life did the same to me. Whether one journeys down the poems like *Heights of Life*, I Inquire… Rain or any other piece, one will have to read once again to understand the poet's mind. Lines such as "Music is yours, Rain/You whisper/We hear" give a philosophical touch to the poem; "emotional mutiny" touches the soul as much as "The thought lies in/Where I fell." "Rooming my tension/In the lap of solitude" makes you wonder.

Not only subtle and lucid but also modernist, this book dives into the different shades of existence, leaving an indelible and poignant mark on the reader's mind.

I will leave the rest to the readers to journey through these poems and give their own verdict.

Bob D' Costa

3rd September, 2015
Kolkata, India

Bob D' Costa is a poet, author, educationist and creative writing instructor. Author of four books of poems, two novels in paperback, three in ebook. Giving poetry readings at home and abroad, Bob conducts writing tours for writers. Besides being a member of Asia Pacific Writers and Translators as well as of FOSWAL, the Apex Body of SAARC, Bob is the Founder and Editor of Whatabook, a publishing house.

Introduction

"I voice the words lined up on my tongue"— yes, the idea to voice harks back to the nascent days of my feeling words in literature, and filling literature with words. Any written form of expression, to me at least, comes as literature. Despite the caress of ma and mollycoddling of baba, a tension housed in my psyche— of being in between my vision and growing experience. Studying had always been my favourite haunt. I have got to manage books in galore. They are my friends who wink at and peep my world through. Gradually it came to my senses that the World is what I create around, and the earth is somewhere I stand upon. I turned flabbergasted. People started anchoring in my life and toyed with me as they wished, and deserted me as they pleased. Therefore worldly friends came lessening. And the urge to unburden my notes of realisation stood tumultuous. Then one day I harboured in an idea through a History book that an individual cannot change a society and its mental make-up; he can do so by putting down the felt record only. So are the diverse subjects—so is Literature—so is mankind—so am I. I clicked the idea and wanted it to flash...yes, I have to write. But to express all I feel, a good vocabulary and a supreme command over language is a must. Surprisingly enough, despite having a poor knowledge of English it came naturally, though haltingly, as a language of my soul. As if a child is craving to get unmasked from a womb. From then on my journey began, to fight against the impediments of learning English.

The train of thoughts and look-outs could easily led me to become a raconteur. But my sheer view experienced not something flat, rather an avalanche speeding down through my pen, unstoppable, rolling and melting, leaving a scary mark. So I opted for poetry to deliberate and deliver as well. *Heights of Life* is my debut collection of 34 short English verses. The poems it contains are selected and trimmed down from my casket of scribbling.

Before or after glancing over the poems, one might wonder about the influences that shaped my thoughts in writing poems. Actually a poem has no language, it is a rhythm of liveliness that has all the vibrations of the universe. I also think that one cannot learn to write poems, its as natural as music. I write my way, somebody writes his way. Notwithstanding, fewer modern Bengali poets whose poetic acumen moved me were: Binoy Majumdar, Shakti Chattopadhyay, and Shankhya Ghosh. I should refer to the name, that, also is the answer of that question I have been tortured with seldom by my students, "Sir, Who is your favourite English poet?" He is someone whose rendition familiarises me with the true sense of the term 'poetry', and also he is someone whom I make out easily i.e. John Keats.

It underwent a torrent of stress and strain to overcome the difficulties in getting this book published from Kolkata, staying back all the way long at Raiganj, North Dinajpur. Especially in a time when the lure and folk-talks of securing a job hovers in one's existence, paving the threshold there somebody supported my decision to pamper the sound and fury of my desire (signifying almost nothing for most of the people I am familiar and also surrounded with). She is Titir Banerjee, my beloved lady, the best gift I have ever got in my life.

Heights of life is an attempt to recapture spent moments through poetry. Here the subtleties of multifaceted time are whispered. I find a poet's job is to let others experience the unseen and the unknown. His is the view of an Everyman. I feel that I envision the nuances of daily life that slowly passes. My duty, therefore, is of a diarist, to note the changes, see the upcoming, and put all these down in my record, to serve mankind ages after. My poems are wide open to multiple interpretations. It is the readers only who will determine the fate and face of Heights of Life. I wish them all a very enjoyable reading.

Tanmoy Bhattacharjee
Raiganj ,West Bengal, India
1st September, 2015

Acknowledgements

I blow the breeze of my sincere acknowledgement to the People who hold my hand (directly or supportively) in actualising my wish and materialising this book.

I have fathered this book with the help of my Publisher, Shri Bitan Chakraborty, who played the mother-figure in getting this book born perfectly. I owe some share of my effort to this person who bothered (though not bothered at all) my frequent calls, and calmly managed everything...he is one who stamped my poetry, in making a mere name into a poet.

Even my absent being bows before Dr. Kiriti Sengupta (Dada), a name easily reckoned by the contemporary readers and writers of Indian English Literature. It is his constant support only that cemented my conviction and doubled the velocity of my persistence. For us, distance has always been of place, not of space.

I must admit the name of Modhura Bandyopadhyay, (an Assistant Professor of English) whose spellbinding illustrations share the credit of my poems in twining the gusto of the entire book *Heights of Life*. With quite a not-wanting-any-credit discomfiture, she tortured her eyes and hands relentlessly, just to shape my thoughts into a perpetual stay. Kudos Modhura! Blessed to have you as my friend.

I register my heartfelt thanksgiving to the following people who retained their faith in my poems and not only they recorded their genuine impressions, but ended up suggesting the notes of improvement for furtherance:

Sudeep Sen   Don Martin   Seshu Chamarty
Anjana Basu   Gopal Lahiri   Bishnupada Ray
Anindya Sekhar Purakayastha   Arka Chattopadhyay
Bob D'Costa

My pen harps on the last name, as Mr. Bob D'Costa, (a very renowned poet among the literati of Calcutta) has been a very darling person to bother about writing the foreword of my book. I never met him personally, nor did I have his contact details. I only heard about his stature as a poet and writer. Out of faith in my honest poetry I persuaded him, and I stood stunned with his approval of my very first request.

Finally, some friends-cum-admirers who metamorphosed my 'I' into an 'incredibly you' are:

Pushpendu Sarkar   Subham Dey   Rumpa Podder

I know guys, one day your utmost belief would push me to staircase the pinnacle of my dream.

Table of Contents

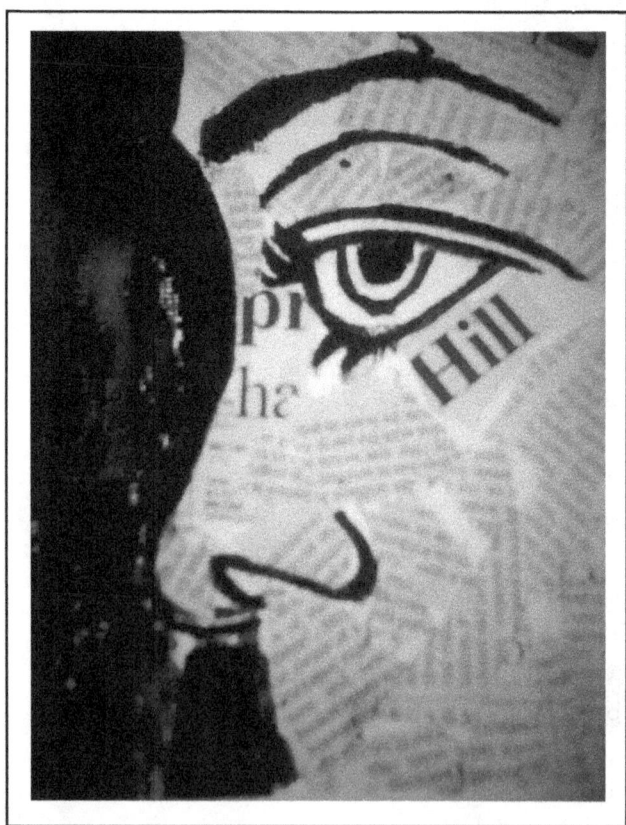

Heights Of Life

I voice the words
Lined up on my tongue
I try the views I have inherited.
To weather each my storm
My efforts are wheeling above

Hardly did I have any win
Tears well up ... sometimes
I am not used to.
My appeals are worded enough.
It's been whiled away, although
My smiles are tutored now,
And wishes stationed.

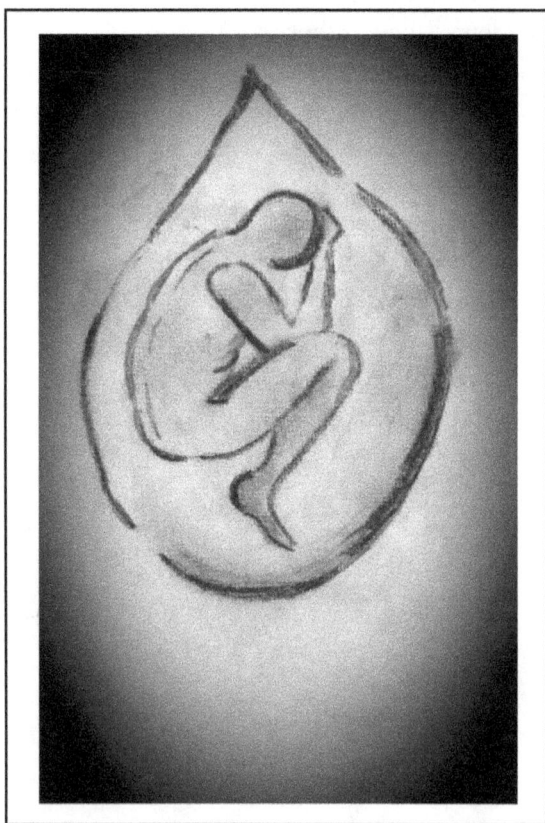

Droplets

A glass of cold water
reminds me sense
of my skin
the droplets touch
my palmy lines,

The nerves inside
summon blood
to give cognizance
Meanwhile she caught me
red-handed
yes, drops on my lifeline...

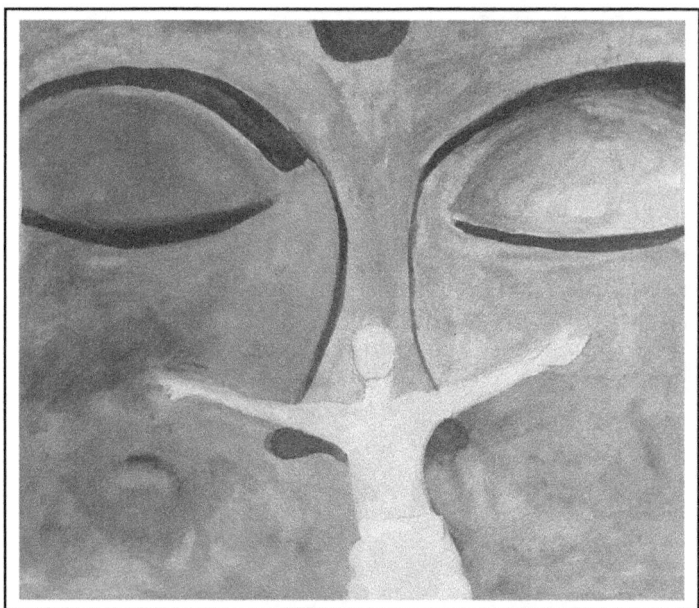

I Inquire ... Rain

Music is yours, Rain.
You whisper
We hear
While oneness with earth
You make prosody
Of all the lives within
While you cry
We smile
But when we cry
Where are you, Rain?

Barren lands find meaning
You propel roots and fruits
But who will wash away
The filth of mind?
Let your drops be
Enlivening

The poem was published in Tuck magazine
[http://tuckmagazine.com/2015/09/22/poetry-84/]

Mind

I am the mind
Do you know me?
I reside in you
Cry in loss, smile in hope

I am the mind
Do you know me?
I reside in you
I pain, I feel
I love, I leave

I am the mind
Do you know me?
I reside in you
I hide, I heal
I mourn, I kill

I am the mind

I Need A Call

Well if you need
Call me once
At least
and then call me
By my name.
Ah, I need not any
Clarion call
Recall that genetic history
Of the earth,
That thick-skinned sentiment
All those pell-mell
And my possessiveness...

I would obviate
The need
For your waning faith.
Forget not
Just become
As we used to
I am afraid
If the
No-win situation still persists.
I am changed now
Totally
My sensations are
Less vapid lately
I would suffice all
Your obsessions
Please redial
For the last time

Listen To The Rational Beggar

Not a penny
Even what I have
I do not have many.
They robbed me off
Not my culture,
Nor destiny,
Neither of my testicles.
But myself.

I am missing.
My self is not in myself.
I consist of ours
They in me, I in them as well
Am I lost, or unfounded?

Hope

Dear me
Come out of the life
Of a match-box.
See there ... nothing
Nothing is lost.
The morning sky so appear
Still...with a vermillion
Listen...
Earth too hear of us
Even carefully
She protects the dewdrops.
See, nothing is lost
Nothing...

Look Back

Do not leave
Not a step ahead
Neither an inch
If left even come back
Be with me, don't move
Neither, never, nowhere
Nor if one gives you a call
Nor be tempted to the colours
Get them straightway dismissed
Hold my fingers
Get cocooned in my body
Get my near, feel my breath
but never foot ahead
Nor even if one dares or threats
Not if you are torn apart

Memories In Monsoon

Greet you monsoon,
This time too
You let it wet
Soaked, dried, and withered
A sweet smell rushes
So does the memory
Gets me back to the past.

It is when both of us
from head to toe
The chase of wild love begins
As if
A bull, refusing the barrier
Intends to meet with infinity
Meet close

Mighty Time

Ruthless temperament of time
With its villainous vigour
Thrust me out
In the abyss of chaos
It spoils my serenity of existence

The weeping confusion prevails
Up to the emotional mutiny.
I watch over the 'watch'
The moment strikes much
The polestar hovers in uncertainty.

To regain the 'again' of that time
Let love be the bemoaning keepsake.

Musings

I have not slept
For many days
Rooming my tension
In the lap of
Solitude.
Will weep one day
For sure
Quenching all the thirst.

I shall forge ahead
Although
Pulling and pushing Continues.
Guarding the threshold
Awaits my man
He otherwise wishes to be
One woman's man.

I shall move
I shall supersede
I shall be back even.

I shall come back
playing
I shall come back
living
I shall come back
musing

My Being Revisited

Come dear ... after ages you have come
Wonder, where to let you sit on
This is my small room, difficult
To head up for a tall man.
Surrounded by people although
Readily at a hand's stretch

See dear, this is my flowery fence,
The floral bushes
Sunlight visits here, everyday
The first streak of daylight.
Birds' chirpings add to the aroma.

Come, and see dear
My first independent look
The memory of my first triumph
My maiden misdeed
Monsoon appears as a guest, and
Drops nectar in my dream-filled sleep.

This is my age-story
It's time to leave the platform now.

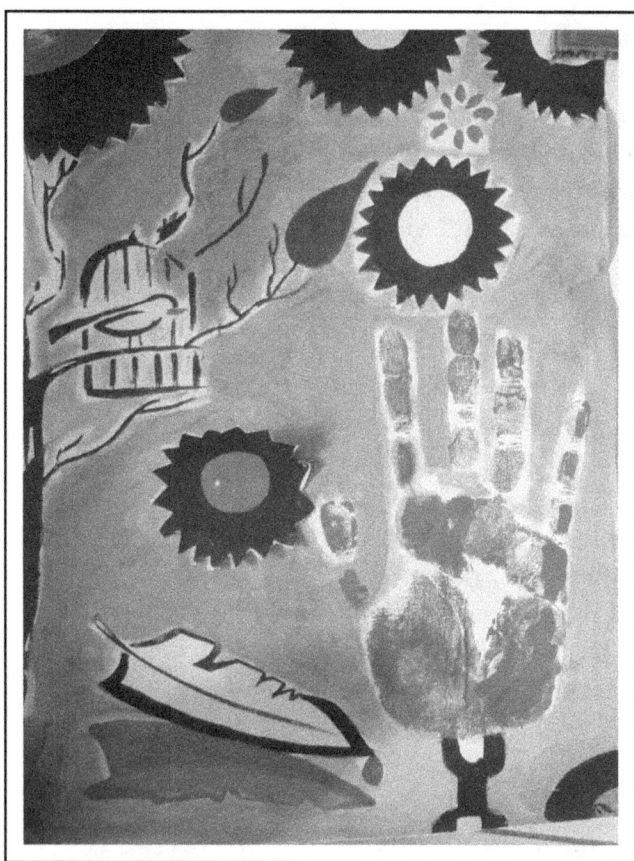

Manacle

A bit light, a bit of thatch
I don't expect anymore.
Few memories well-left
Few moments well-spent
Nothing more I can see.
Heated cooking-place,
Unguarded bathing,
A glass of cold water.

What else can I give you?
Take care, go home safe
Don't wear the manacle.

Nocturnal Vision

Coming across the invisible molehills
Along with the earthly secretions
I suck
Withered are my eyelids
Do not haste, open up
The unfolded Canopy
Casements catch thoughts
Overpowered by the lunatic lacuna
The arteries get moistened.
Futile to be in a coherent whole

The sperm sees still nudity
Arise, beware
My night is drunk
Its trembled hours
Silently passes on my indolence.

Painter

Do you know the painter?
The one who
Portrays the bleak and
Gloomy picture
Of the human predicament?
His brush
Is devoid of logic.
He delineates too...
Sarcastically.
He paints
Our every now.
His variegated colours
Penetrate into
The impassable mental chasm.

You may go on
Up to his instructions.
I am out of the game.
No borders are there
No order even.
When my salty waters groan

He says
"Stop howling you know-nothing"

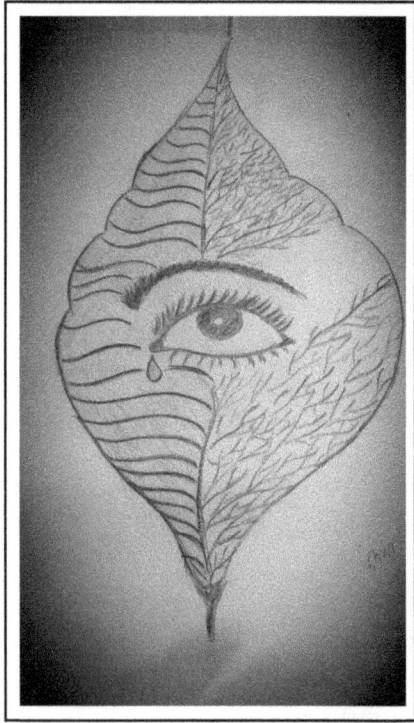

Pain In Pleasure

Pain and Pleasure
Frown at times
With allures and lullabies
And they really bother
If I fail
To look back at them

Sometimes I wonder
how don't
they stop oozing sweat;
even blood
if sought to get me
through my life-ordeal

I find pleasure in pain,
For it is devised
To divulge glee

My ever-awe-struck eyelids
Find Close match
To causal rotation

But the glossy corners
Fail to locate the swift
And the twists in my smile

I consider pain
To be an enabler,

Not a constraint
The end is scaled...
Pleasure continues to baffle
In smoky perfume.

The poem was published in the Vol. 1, Issue 2
(September 2015) of the The Literary Herald : An
Internationally Refereed English e-Journal

Portrait

I try to find reason in the tears.
The eyeball mirrors mismatch

A reflection of misery

The glossy neck-chain

Is transparent in bondage.

Wait, look at
The crunched nipple zone.

It fails to arouse my glands

The mother-breast is not
Miser in providing
Rather
In producing growth-sap.

The baby might be acting

In letting us know
How benevolent the mother is.

So is he posing to suck

Hiding his hunger?

Soliloquy

My hunger clings to the root
That contains water
Although my thirst turns
Ungratified.

So you are leaving
Well you may;
Shall not call you back
If you are free to forget
Me as a past, why not I
Forgive you and
Head towards tomorrow?

Quest

Woman and man
Two edges of a leaf;

Life ... the wanderer
Ever confusing.
Who loves whom
When why where?

Life ... the audacious
Dare not to die.
The answer is vague
Forever
In quest of why

Split Woman

Colourless drops of life
Shall I want
But who dares
To provide me life-sap?
Looters went on sucking.
Although
The blood remains within
That's too impure.

Water floats
Water feeds
Water fills
So my life is drowned.

They squeezed my breast,
Sucked my shame
Still my eyes are dried
Still ... my body seeks water.

The Journey Begins

Memories lost
At the showery drops.
Let the rain brim
The lake of life.
Nostalgia pleads
To fumble my own life
In the crowded flow
Of the brimmed water.

Back-To-Back

Nothing at the back
A haunt at the back
An open field only

Void is at the back
At the back, a bug scratching the brain

Undone, misfit deeds at the back
Sobbing at the back
Lane-by-lanes at the back
Although nothing is at the back

All yet to get in front

Observations In Rhapsodies

1

See, there is coming
The husky whisper
Two robust hands,
Stiff, close-posed
Nearing your throat
The distance is hard
To measure, but
The destination is fixed
Fearful ...
Of the throttling grip
But you
Cannot return

You are a soul,
You have a body ... borrowed

2

There was a time when I used to
My emotions died, feelings dried
Metaphors stuck to
Past never dies, it kills
And makes all changes to skills

Past strikes unbending
My life, with its last lingering look
I was told in whispers
Not to violate any modes, but
To decode the shackles

My know-nothing mind still rambles
My years are stricken, I agree
With thoughts rotten, senses burdened

Strife-torn past rendered my today

Let me opt for a comeback...

3

The city is in trance, while
The hungry grave in slumber
Time prepares a scapegoat
And my Scaffold howls in hurry

Preparation still prepares
Two seers gaze
One from above, the other
Still in a fix

4

Respected Tyrant!
Did you realize last day
The magical trick of power,
Unjust in the guise of just?
You kill people, so what?
They have never been your
Kith and Kin
You are absolutely alright
Bloodless, untainted, guarded

I am no more
Do what you wish now
...

I don't trust you

5

Society…I need u
If I exist anymore
Society…I mean u
 If you are meant ever
Society…I feel u
For those musings
My heart bore
Of you, your, yours
Society…I defy
Know not why

6

Once I picked a quarrel
With a prosperous loser
But hardly had he said this...
I mean protest
He should have been,
With sticks and spears

Had I been there,
I would have retorted this way

In-Between

Walking beneath the stars
Muddy road, nudity,
When the basic instincts rise
The thought lies in where I fell
My wants tantalise
Night has its terms too...
I agree, that I exist

I shall be born again
few hours left

Unwordiness

The past and present
Both are spiteful
Differences are blatant than
The ready mental make-up.
Those sunny days
Remind me of the weapons
Verbal, premature
Though strong yet.
Of scruple
My thought was; terrified
Now my being is, resulting
In the denial.
Scrolling down
The last canvas,
My nip is broken down
Unable to gather so
The pulse and beat
The search is on
Or may have gone.

Speak Out Volcano

Speak, speak, o dear volcano!
You are not tongue-tied
You have your vigour too
Emit, if you cannot erupt
You know, my neighbours
Fear a simple tumour
Allow them to see you pass
Convince them that
 The fire is my friend.

I miss you badly, o volcano!
Since the last blow and flow
The burning sensation continues

I want to see the safari once more.

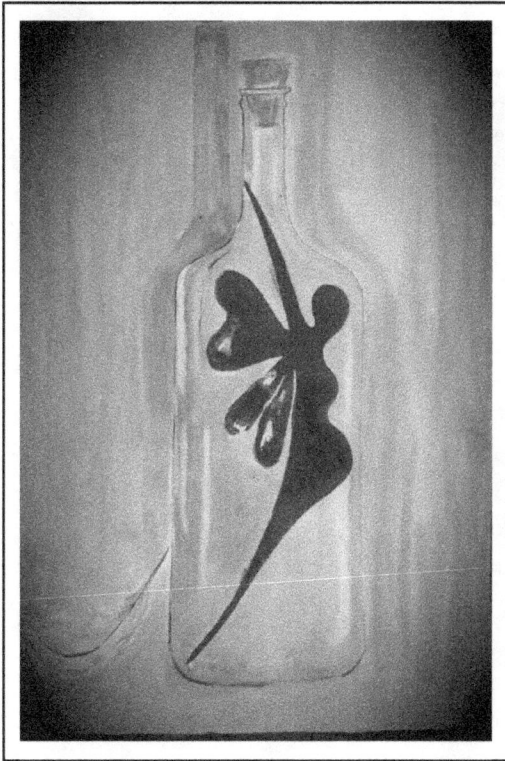

Woman

She is not woman
She is female
The second sex
Unsung muses they have become.

An essential commodity.
Victim of acid bulb.
Victim of co-dying.
She is in exotic chains
Although
In their hand
Is the bobbin of freedom.

They live the life
Of caterpillar
Turning into myopic bacteria.

They are being deflowered,
Every other day,
Time and again,
All the same.

Once in womb
Memory being deleted
Men matter to womb
They batter to womb even
Vagina will witness,

The hearing
That is on the day next.

Progress being throttled.
Honour still unbottled.

We Shall Overcome

Dear earth,
Slow shaking down.
The roots and fruits
Come from your within.
You are the kind soil.
You germinate sprout
Women give birth.
We evolved likewise
Promisingly...
But now you changed
Your liking...from greenery
To debris, dust, rust.
We left long past, the
Phase of land-division. But
You made us reminisce.
Can you hear, earth
The moaning and groaning appeal?
Can you see the child
Peeping from lifeless articles?
We have to reappear
Is that you learnt us once.
People must rejuvenate
Your evolution only tells that.
Stay tranquil, dear earth.
Hope soon the nectar of our peace
Would pacify your breach
Your movement...

Graveyard

The husky groan of the leaves
Are coming
A lonely mother bereaves…
She benights the fervent hopes,
And prowess of her son.
Shedding tears
Over the Lifeless white.
Pieces of red fragrance
Shrunken overtly.
With poor eyeshot
She plunges into
The other tombs.

…The last embrace

The poem was published in Tuck magazine
[http://tuckmagazine.com/2015/09/22/poetry-84/]

What People Are Saying...

"This exquisite little volume is a fine debut work by an emerging Indian poet. The poems, while not lengthy, are rich with well-crafted images, textures, and nuances. Just about all subjects are covered, some in a serious vein and others with a lighter tone. All readers will find things they are well familiar with, and with which they can identify. This book is a welcome addition to English-language Indian poetry, and is a must-have for any serious poetry-lover's bookshelf."

— Don Martin
best-selling author, editor, blogger and
critic based in Tucson, Arizona,USA

"Heights of Life by Tanmoy Bhattacharjee is literally about his poems which are filled with passion and ooze biographical titbits real or imaginary. They overwhelm the readers in an interesting way. Things deeply felt in one's life leave a scar or sweet impression on the person's psyche. The poet writes his lines as if engaged in a dialogue with a long gone person infusing some cross images that pop up now, more when we least expect. The tenor of the poems makes an interesting reading. His analogies and imagery arrest reader's attention. Three poems bowled me over. They are: 1) I Inquire ... Rain, 2) Look Back and 3) Soliloquy. The internal debate, love/hate/ philosophizing life to the point of hurting oneself should make any one to sit up and lap

up the racy contents. All the best to the promising poet. Can't help quoting one gem: "...Music is yours, Rain./ You whisper We hear /While oneness with earth /You make prosody Of all the lives within /While you cry We smile/But when we cry/Where are you, Rain?""

-Seshu Chamarty
Poet, Translator & Critic, Hyderabad

"Tanmoy Bhattacharya is one of the most promising young poets currently writing in English. His debut collection *Heights of Life* steers a clear and thoughtful path through the various images of life. He writes more from his heart and his poems are emotive and examine human concerns against the inner workings of the soul. Another important aspect is the brevity of his poems. Looking forward to read more poems from this young and passionate poet."

— Gopal Lahiri
Earth Scientist, Poet & Critic, Mumbai

"Perhaps in every consistent poet's development there happens a crisis, a crisis of faith, about his art and life. This marks his grappling and coming to terms with an idiom of expression, and a transition to maturity. This new collection of poems titled *Heights of Life* by Tanmoy Bhattacharjee can best be described as poetry of transition towards his coming to terms with a poetic idiom and eventual poetic maturity. Hope this collection will mark a significant phase of his poetic career and find a place in his overall oeuvre."

—Bishnupada Ray
currently an Associate Professor (Dept. Of English), North Bengal University, Siliguri...He is a Nationally recognised Poet and Critic.

"Tanmoy's poetic animadversions in this new book testify his brilliant interlocutions at what Heidegger while musing on poetry called *apophansis*. The rudimentary and the quotidian glisten through his meditative renderings while achieving the rare kinship between *techne* and *poiesis*. Marleau Ponty's insistence that "Being requires creation of us" stands substantiated through this budding poet's sense of depth and modes of defamiliarization. While he maps both the agony and ecstasy of life, his singular *labenswelt* or his densely crafted *Gestalt* in his imaginative outpourings enframe a unique cartography of introspection."

—Dr. Anindya Sekhar Purakayastha
Associate Professor, dept. Of English,
Kaji Nazrul University, Asansol, West Bengal, India

"These are intimate communications. When a voice is slowly turning itself into a murmur, all speech becomes a demand for love. Tanmoy's calm and contained articulations express such a demand. They toy with this demand by insisting on recuperation: "See nothing is lost/Nothing..." These dewdrop-protected utterances etch a line of flight that encourages the readers to come out of their cocoons and open up the unseen petals of life. The appeal to "enliven" that runs through these poems like a stitch of time quilts them into a haunting haunt. These heartfelt expressions will melt the snow of words with the warmth of affect as they waver in scale from varying heights of life through the undulating valleys of love, culminating in the final haven of a graveyard where life and death are knotted in infinity. I hope Tanmoy's readers feel the love he has put into his breathing words. Best wishes to *Heights of Life*."

—Arka Chattopadhyay
Academic & Doctoral Candidate, Writing and Society,
University of Western Sydney, Australia

www.ingramcontent.com/pod-product-compliance
Lightning Source LLC
Chambersburg PA
CBHW020606030426
42337CB00013B/1232